Far had we come and long had we traveled, from Scotland, Ukraine, Korea, China, France, Japan, North America—from north.

We had flown as far south as we could go, and boarded our ship in Punta Arenas, Chile. We had barely entered the fearsome Drake Passage when a stormy blast threw a scientist from his berth, breaking his bones. The ship turned back, to the nearest point in Argentina, to send him to a hospital, then home back north, to Boston.

Six days ago, we left the cliffs of Tierra del Fuego—the foot of South America—behind us. Since then our ship's bow, and our faces, turned only south. Now, at last, the captain said, we were near. Near what? The portholes showed only gloom, thick dark cloud that hid any hint of destination.

We passed the radar dot of Brabant Island and turned into the Gerlache Strait, a deep groove of sea along the Antarctic Peninsula. Gray. Mist. Fog. Cloud. Moving on south.

"Let's go out on deck," said Pete. I followed him, with the other scientists on our team: Paty and Carlton. We pulled on thick parkas, quilted trousers and heavy boots, over layers of warmer, thinner clothes, and faced the cold wet outside.

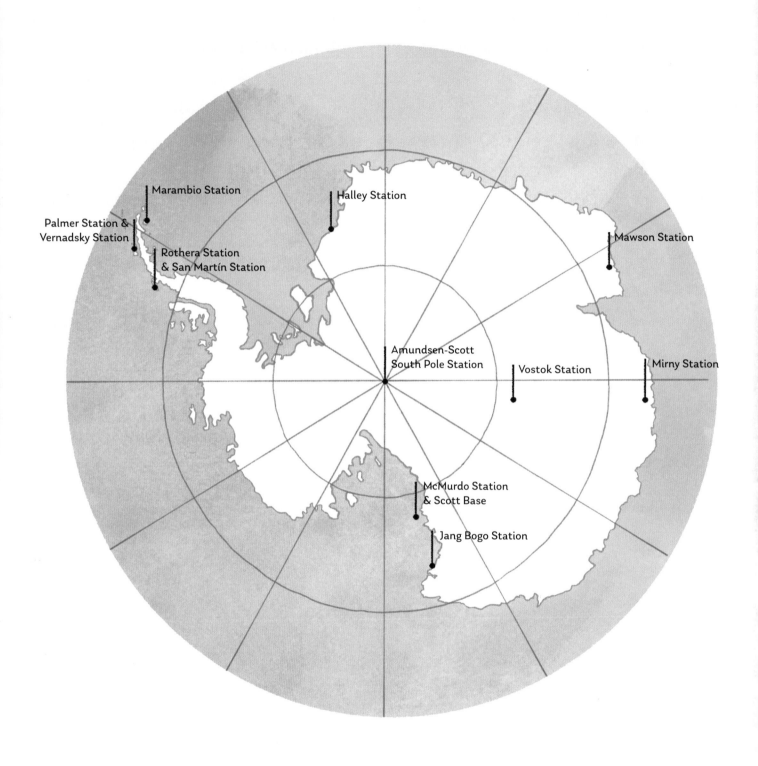

Marambio Station

Palmer Station &
Vernadsky Station

Rothera Station
& San Martín Station

Halley Station

Mawson Station

Amundsen-Scott
South Pole Station

Vostok Station

Mirny Station

McMurdo Station
& Scott Base

Jang Bogo Station

ANTARCTICA
THE MELTING CONTINENT

By **Karen Romano Young**

Illustrated by
Angela Hsieh

What on Earth Books

For Pete Countway – KRY

For my mom, whose love of travel let me see the world – AH

What on Earth Books is an imprint of What on Earth Publishing
Allington Castle, Maidstone, Kent ME16 0NB, United Kingdom
30 Ridge Road Unit B, Greenbelt, Maryland, 20770, United States

First published in the United States in 2022

Written by Karen Romano Young
Illustrated by Angela Hsieh
Staff for this book: Patrick Skipworth, Editor; Andy Forshaw, Designer
Book and print production: Booklabs.co.uk

ISBN: 978-1-913750-53-4

Printed in India RP/Haryana-India/11/2021

10 9 8 7 6 5 4 3 2 1

whatonearthbooks.com

CONTENTS

INTRODUCTION

I'd never sensed such deep stillness. Only the thrumming of the ship's engine and the hissing of icy waters could be heard. Passing through fields of ice chunks and broken-up icebergs, we peered into the foggy veil. Was anything there?

Suddenly a ray of sun broke through, then another. A patch of blue sky, then another. Within minutes, the ship chugged out of the low cloud into the most incredible panorama I'd ever seen: foaming aquamarine sea, floating icebergs layered with all the blues of heaven and earth, walled in by monumental white mountains that seemed to exhale sprites of icy wind. And—there!—the spouts of humpback whales, fellow migrants from the north. They'd come all the way from equatorial waters to feed in Antarctica. And—there!—a flock of Adélie penguins "flying" through the water, arcing like dolphins. Everyone broke out in smiles; I burst into tears: here at last!

Pete leaned over my shoulder, pointing out what looked like a thin stick at the foot of a mountain. "That's a British weather station," he said. The "stick" was an antenna the size of a city skyscraper, our only clue to the scale of the mountains that surrounded the Strait.

It was my first lesson in understanding Antarctica: how huge it is and how hard to size up. That and the slogan people are always saying: "It's a harsh continent." They mean, be careful here. They mean, we are very far from help. They mean, this environment is not designed to be hospitable to humans. On the contrary, it often seems to be designed to destroy us. And yet, the future of Antarctica's ice—so vital to maintaining our planet's balance— depends more than anything on our actions.

Chapter 1
THE UNKNOWN LAND

Today, Antarctica is Earth's most inhospitable continent, the coldest and driest place on the planet. Only a handful of plant and animal species survive here. But Antarctica used to be different: Not cold. Not isolated. Not a deathtrap. At one time, Antarctica was ice free and covered instead in—wait for it—dinosaurs!

The remains of dinosaurs have been unearthed in Antarctica since the 1960s and are still being discovered today. The oldest among them lived during the early Triassic period, 250 to 245 million years ago; these were the same species of dinosaur as those found on other continents—because in early dinosaur times pieces of Antarctica were joined to other pieces of land to form much larger continents than those we have today. Later species were particular to Antarctica, showing that Antarctica had separated from the other continents by this time, causing those later dinosaurs to adapt to the now-unique environment. These included relatives of *Brachiosaurus* and *Titanosaurus*, but, unlike the giant examples found in other parts of the world, the Antarctic species were as small as retriever dogs.

In early dinosaur times and before, Antarctica wasn't even here, at the very bottom of the world. All of Earth's continents ride atop plates that make up the planet's outer layer, called its crust, and are constantly moving. These plates glide over molten rock heated by energy from the center of Earth. This motion is incredibly slow: at its quickest it's about as fast as your fingernails grow. As the plates move, continents crash into each other, new lands are created, and other land sinks under the water. Today, Antarctica is made up of West Antarctica and East Antarctica. And how each of them ended up at the bottom of the world is a different story.

East Antarctica was once part of a large continent called Gondwana, as were Africa, India, Australia, and South America. But Gondwana began to break up around 200 million years ago, and the part that became East Antarctica eventually became more solid, stable, and frozen than the land that makes up West Antarctica today. Among its secrets is a buried mountain range, the Gamburtsev Mountains, hidden under the East Antarctic ice sheet. During the Jurassic period 180 million years ago (the middle of dinosaur times), the movement of the continents pushed East Antarctica south. Eventually, over the next 100 million years, it shifted to its current position over the South Pole. As East Antarctica moved south, it slid over another plate and, where the crust sank, lava bubbled up in volcanoes. This formed both the Andes Mountain range that runs the length of South America and the Antarctic Peninsula (the long arm extending northward).

West Antarctica developed later, in the Cretaceous period (the end of the dinosaur times), around 100.5 million years ago, when shards of an uplifting plate split into pieces. You can see those same forces are still at work today in active volcanoes, including Mount Erebus, which towers, smoldering, over Antarctic research stations that edge the Ross Sea.

As the massive pieces of Antarctica's puzzle—East and West Antarctica—crunched together at the bottom of the world, a channel of ocean broke through the thinning strip of land that still connected the Antarctic Peninsula to the southern tip of South America and formed the Drake Passage. Now Antarctica was separated from the other continents, and a current of cold water—known as the Antarctic Circumpolar Current—formed a ring around it, forever cutting Antarctica off from warmer seas. In "just" 20 million years, Antarctica froze.

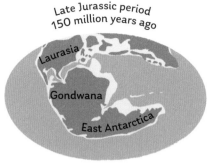

Late Jurassic period
150 million years ago

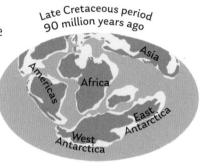

Late Cretaceous period
90 million years ago

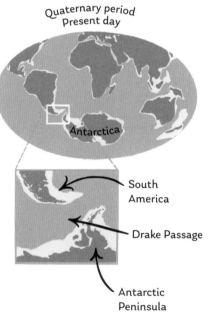

Quaternary period
Present day

Antarctica

South America

Drake Passage

Antarctic Peninsula

WHAT MOTION?
The motion of plates, known as plate tectonics, is ongoing. Millions of years in the future, the shapes and sizes of Earth's continents will have changed again.

MOUNTAINS OF LAND UNDER MOUNTAINS OF ICE

Antarctica may be covered in ice today, but beneath most of it is solid ground. In some places the underlying rock stays hidden under massive glaciers; in others it breaks through as towering mountains. Elsewhere, the ice presses out from the shore and over the ocean in huge sheets directly above the water.

The Antarctic Peninsula extends into the Southern Ocean. It is over 620 miles (1,000 km) across the Drake Passage from its tip to the closest point in South America— Tierra del Fuego in Chile.

Between East and West Antarctica loom the 2,000 mile (3,220 km) Transantarctic Mountain range, which looks like peaks peeking out of the snow but are really a towering range almost the height of the Rocky Mountains in North America.

TRANSANTARCTIC MOUNTAINS

WEST ANTARCTICA

Antarctica's average elevation is 8,200 feet (2,500 m), making it the highest continent. The highest point above sea level on the icecap is in East Antarctica at 13,428 feet (4,093 m). The highest mountain, where rock breaks through the ice, is Mount Vinson at 16,050 feet (4,892 m).

Mount Erebus is the most active volcano in Antarctica. Inside its crater is a glowing lake of lava.

The East Antarctic Ice Sheet and West Antarctic Ice Sheet are the two biggest ice sheets in the world. The thickest point of the East Antarctic Ice Sheet, which is the larger of the two, is nearly 3 miles (4,776 m) thick—over fifty times as tall as the Statue of Liberty.

West   East

EAST ANTARCTICA

The South Pole is at the most southern point on Earth, in the middle of Antarctica.

What's the Antarctic low point? An enormous crater 300 miles (482 km) wide, which lies 1 mile (1.6 km) under Wilkes Land, part of the East Antarctic Ice Sheet. It was created by an asteroid estimated to have smashed into Earth 250 million years ago.

The crater is twice the size of the one created by the Chicxulub asteroid that's thought to have wiped out the non-avian dinosaurs (the ones not related to birds) 65 million years ago.

LAKE VOSTOK

ANTARCTIC LOW POINT

ICE VOCABULARY

- **BERGY BITS** – broken up icebergs

- **BRASH ICE** – floating chunks of ice up to 6 ft 6 in (2 m) wide that form when other bits of ice break up

- **CALVING** – the breaking away of a giant chunk of ice from the edge of a glacier

- **FIRN** – dense, granular ice that forms as snow ages and compresses as the air is squeezed out of it

- **FRAZIL** – soft ice that forms in turbulent water

- **GLACIER** – a river of moving ice formed over many years as falling snow compresses

- **GROWLERS** – small icebergs or big blocks of ice that float underwater and pose an invisible danger to boats

- **ICE SHEET** – a huge, permanent layer of ice covering land

- **ICE SHELF** – a floating sheet of ice attached to land

- **ICEBERG** – a chunk of glacier that calves off and gets carried out to sea

- **NILAS** – thick, sludgy ice that forms as salt water freezes

- **PACK ICE** – an expanse of sea ice made up of lots of smaller pieces that drift because of wind or water

- **PANCAKE ICE** – disks of ice that form when wind blows through sludgy ice

Most of Antarctica may be covered in ice and snow, but the driest spots on Earth are also found here. The McMurdo Dry Valleys receive less than 3.9 inches (100 mm) of precipitation per year.

FROM ICE HOUSE TO GREENHOUSE

Before the Southern Ocean tied its cold knot around Antarctica, conditions there were pleasant enough not just for dinosaurs but for many other warmth-loving forms of life. Ferns and freshwater fish, snails and sharks all flourished there. But once the cold loop of the Antarctic Circumpolar Current closed around the continent, snow fell, ending those warmer conditions. Over eons, snow accumulated on Antarctica's surface, compressed into layer upon layer of ice, and began its ongoing slide to the sea in the form of frozen rivers called glaciers. When a glacier reaches the sea, it "calves"—yes, like a cow—into smaller pieces which fall into the water. These pieces are called icebergs. They melt as they move away from land, floating north across the ocean. Their melting affects sea levels worldwide.

Antarctica's glaciers have melted and refrozen, melted and refrozen, as Earth has warmed and cooled in natural rhythms. Take the Pleistocene era, which began 2.6 million years ago, for example. It was the start of a series of up-and-down temperature swings that caused Earth to freeze and thaw in 40,000-year cycles, following a pattern created by Earth's orbit around the Sun. Right now, Earth is in another ice age—the latest "Ice House" period—which began when the Pleistocene ended, 11,700 years ago. The glaciers we see today have been building up and sliding down into the ocean in a delicate balance since then—until recently.

Since the mid-20th century, Earth has been steadily warming. The cause of this change started earlier, during the Industrial Revolution. This period, which began in about 1760, marks the moment when engines fed by fossil fuels—coal, oil and natural gas—began to be used for heat and power. When fossil fuels are burned, gases called carbon dioxide,

Calving glacier

methane, and nitrous oxide are produced. Human activities, such as farming and disposing of waste in landfills, also create these gases, and they all began to build up in Earth's atmosphere. These "greenhouse gases" have created a blanket effect that continues to warm Earth today. They keep the cold out and heat in. This increases water vapor in Earth's atmosphere—clouds and rain—adding further to what's called the greenhouse effect.

While all of this has been going on, the glaciers in Antarctica have continued to grind into the seabed and slide out over the ocean as ice shelves. The warming sea nibbles upward and the glaciers flow downward. In a balanced system, iceberg calving balances with the snowfall, so new ice is created at the same rate as it falls into the ocean. But now, the greenhouse effect is accelerating glacial melting, and the snowfall on top can't keep up with the calving below, so an excess of icebergs are calving into the sea.

Antarctica's glaciers are storehouses for Earth's fresh water. As the glaciers melt, sea levels are rising, sinking coastlines and making them part of the sea. Worldwide, people and their burning of fossil fuels are causing global warming and sea levels to rise. In Antarctica, scientists are rushing to learn about the past to help everyone understand what's happening now and what could happen, for better or worse, in the future. If Antarctic ice shrinks, what will happen to the rest of the world? But, wait. The question, scientists say, is not *If*. It's *When?* and *How soon? How much? How fast?* Humans in Antarctica are working to find out. But we are still new to this continent; there is much to learn, and time is tight.

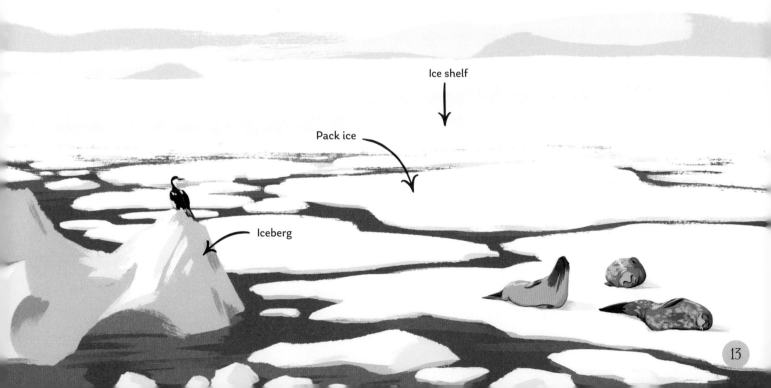

Ice shelf

Pack ice

Iceberg

HEROES IN AN UNKNOWN LAND

For most of human history, nobody went to Antarctica. Nobody even knew that Antarctica was there. Some mapmakers, lacking data, penciled in a land mass labeled *Terra Australis Incognita*: the "unknown southern land" at the far end of the world.

Antarctica is the last region on Earth that people discovered. It's possible that Māori people from New Zealand reached Antarctica in the 7th century, but the first individual known to have crossed the the Antarctic Circle—the latitude line 67° South—was Captain James Cook aboard HMS *Resolution*, in 1773. He and his crew never spotted the mainland, just a few islands offshore. In January 1820, a Russian expedition led by Fabian Gottlieb von Bellingshausen and Mikhail Lazarev glimpsed the ice shelf that extends into the sea off the frozen continent. Just three days later, a British expedition led by the Irish captain Edward Bransfield caught sight of the tip of the Antarctic Peninsula, and in November the American seal hunter Nathaniel Palmer sailed in.

Almost 90 years later—once explorers had achieved their goal of reaching the North Pole, and worldwide fame—a period known as the Heroic Age of Antarctic Exploration saw thrilling treks to the coldest and most remote spots on the southern continent. The goal of these men—they were all white men, accompanied by some cats, dogs, and ponies—was to be the first to reach the geographic South Pole. Teams of explorers led by Ernest Shackleton and Robert Falcon Scott of the United Kingdom, Douglas Mawson of Australia, and Roald Amundsen of Norway aspired to win the heroes' race.

While the heroic explorers made observations and recorded data that would help the wider world understand this unknown place, what mattered most to them was the fame that would come from being first to the South Pole and from

WHICH POLE?

The point where the axis pokes through the bottom of the globe is the geographic south pole. Geographic poles are based on lines of latitude. The North Pole is always at 90° North, and the South Pole at 90° South (0° is the Equator). The magnetic poles reflect the entry and exit points of Earth's magnetic force. These points change position, so the magnetic poles do, too.

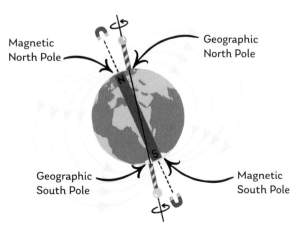

Magnetic North Pole

Geographic North Pole

Geographic South Pole

Magnetic South Pole

Shackleton

On Shackleton's third voyage to Antarctica, his ship *Endurance* became stuck in the ice. The crew spent 10 months trying to free it before it finally sank and they were forced to abandon the expedition.

Mawson

Amundsen

Scott

making it home in one piece. There were many who didn't: scurvy, a vitamin C deficiency disease caused by poor diet; crevasses, huge cracks in the ice; and the fierce cold were among the biggest causes of death. In 1908, during the Nimrod Expedition, Shackleton set the record for travelling the "Furthest South," but bad weather stopped him at 88° 23' South, still 112 miles (180 km) short of the South Pole. The following year, as part of the same expedition, Mawson, along with another Australian and a Scot, reached the magnetic South Pole.

It was Amundsen who planted the first flag at the geographic South Pole on December 14, 1911—Norway's. Thirty-four days later, as Amundsen and his team traveled safely home, Scott reached the South Pole. Waiting for him was a note left by the Norwegian explorer. Scott was devastated to realize that Amundsen had gotten there first. But far worse than coming second, Scott and his entire team died of cold and hunger on the return journey.

THE SEASONS ARE POLAR OPPOSITES

The Sun's position relative to Earth's gives opposite seasons to the northern and southern hemispheres, so Antarctica's summer is December to March.

During the Heroic Expeditions, the explorers—among them, mountaineers, scientists, artists, tradesmen, cooks, and navigators—took the measure of Antarctica, checking air and water temperature and gathering data about the environment. But heroism and being first would continue as the main goal for decades. In 1934, American Admiral Richard E. Byrd, famed for having flown over both the North and South Poles, camped alone on the Ross Ice Shelf for five months, with just the company of his sled dogs and a cow. In 1931, Ingrid Christensen and Mathilde Wegger became the first women to see Antarctica, from aboard a ship. Though Christensen tried to land several times over the next few years, she was unsuccessful until 1937. Two years earlier, in 1935, Caroline Mikkelsen had become the first woman to step onto the coast of the Vestfold Hills in East Antarctica and helped raise a Norwegian flag on a spot now named Ingrid Christensen Land.

In 1956 the U.S. Navy landed the first airplane at the South Pole; the seven men aboard were the first to stand at the South Pole since Scott had been there in 1912. In another important first, a team of women arrived at the South Pole in 1969. They disembarked from their plane arm-in-arm, so none of them could claim to be first.

HOW COLD IS TOO COLD?

Frostbite can occur when the skin gets so cold that fluid in skin cells freezes, eventually killing the cells. Many early polar explorers lost their most vulnerable extremities—tips of noses, cheekbones, fingers and toes—to frostbite. Covering up is key.

Even more serious is hypothermia, a condition caused when it's so cold that the body's core temperature drops. Early signs include the mumbles, stumbles, and fumbles—clumsiness in speech, movement, and coordination. This is because the arms and legs send blood to the vital organs in the core. It can be grumbles, too, as someone with hypothermia will often insist they're fine. A "man overboard" can enter hypothermia in just 12 minutes. The remedy is to remove wet clothes and get the victim warm, even if it means climbing into a sleeping bag with them.

(From left to right) U.S. scientists Lois Jones, Kay Lindsay, Eileen McSaveney, Jean Pearson and Terry Tickhill Terrell, and New Zealand's Pam Young

The McMurdo Dry Valleys, which are reachable only by helicopter, have field camps of tents and permanent structures such as this one.

PARADE OF NATIONS

By Admiral Byrd's time, several countries had claimed control, known as sovereignty, over parts of Antarctica. The nearby nations—Chile, Argentina, New Zealand, and Australia—each wanted to claim the closest land on the continent. The British, whose Empire stretched across the globe, wanted a piece, too. Nations who sailed to certain coasts first—the Norwegians and French—declared those areas as theirs. In 1939, German seaplanes flew over, dropping darts inscribed with Nazi swastikas over thousands of square miles from above to try to claim the land as theirs. Soon after, the U.S. and U.K. established the first bases, and, following World War II, science expeditions took on the dual purpose of claiming territory and conducting research.

These power plays ended in the mid-1950s when an international group of 70 science organizations declared an International Geophysical Year in 1957–58, spanning the Antarctic summer. In 1959, the world united in setting Antarctica aside for two purposes: peace and knowledge. The 12 countries who signed the Antarctic Treaty suspected that the coldest continent contained significant secrets, and that science could best be pursued if nations worked together.

Now there are 54 countries signed up and research stations dotted across the vast snow-covered expanse of Antarctica. Many are jumping-off points to field camps where scientists can shelter for a few weeks in the summer season in tents or other temporary structures.

These scientists are in a hurry to write the history of Antarctica. Everybody working there is in a race against time, a struggle to understand the continent even as it changes right under their feet. What's the rush? Well, Earth's climate is changing much more quickly than ever before, and it's changing fastest of all in Antarctica.

Chapter 2
IN A HURRY TO KNOW

From my drawing desk at the U.S.-run Palmer research station on the edge of the Antarctic Peninsula, I felt, as well as heard, a rumble that shook the floor. I ran to the lab door and looked across Arthur Harbor to the cliff-face of the Marr Ice Piedmont—the foot of the mountainous glacier that slopes up from the coast. With a roar, a calf of ice descended in slow motion, like a slab of icing falling off the side of a birthday cake but much, much bigger and bluer. As the brand-new iceberg met the sea, a foaming wave swept across Arthur Harbor. Over days and weeks the berg would stick around Palmer Station, flowing closer and farther away with the wind, before finally lumbering away from the coast and into the current that would carry it north.

Newborn icebergs from recent calving events loomed near and dotted far along the horizon, shaped like everything from a scallop shell to a Hershey's Kiss to

Bart Simpson's head, and colored in spooky, spacey shades of blue. So many! Too many? Every conversation at Palmer Station involved details of glacier shrinkage. The Marr Ice Piedmont itself continues to thin and pull back from the shore at a rate of 33 feet (10 m) a year, and is now more than a quarter mile (400 m) from its 1960 location. These days in Antarctica, few people try to reach new places or do things first, as they did in the age of heroes. Almost everyone focuses on learning about conditions in Antarctica. It would be impossible to visit this place without realizing something new was going on—and wondering where it would lead.

In February 2020, scientists working at Marambio, Argentina's research station on Seymour Island, experienced something rare: T-shirt weather, 70°F (20.75°C). Marambio station sits at the tip of the Antarctic Peninsula, which has warmed three times faster than the average rate of anywhere else on Earth. Global warming affects the poles more intensely than the tropical zones (near the equator) or temperate zones (between the tropical and polar zones). A 40-year study showed that in 2020 Antarctica sent six times more ice into the sea than it did in 1979, at the start of the study. While the East Antarctic Ice Sheet and Central Antarctica are more stable, currently contributing 30 percent of the total ice melting in Antarctica, the West Antarctic Ice Sheet is undergoing rapid change. It's home to two of the most vulnerable of the world's five key glaciers—the Pine Island Glacier (the PIG) and the Thwaites Glacier. Should they melt, they would cause floods on every continent, raising sea levels by 4 feet (1.2 m) worldwide. The East Antarctic Ice Sheet holds ten times as much ice as the West Antarctic Ice Sheet, a major concern if it were to start to melt more rapidly, too.

WINDOWS TO THE PAST

While I've been writing this book, scientists' findings have flowed in so quickly that it's been hard to keep up. Each finding opens a window to a point along Antarctica's timeline. Here are some of the most incredible recent discoveries and the scientists who uncovered them.

BRIAN ATKINSON AND THE JURASSIC PINE FOREST

Not only was there a forest in Antarctica in dinosaur times, but it contained conifer trees—a group that includes pine trees. When scientist Brian Atkinson, from the University of Kansas, analyzed a 200-million-year-old conifer cone found in the Carapace Nunatak area of the Transantarctic Mountains in Antarctica, he realized that the specimen told the story of a whole new branch of these trees' family tree. <u>Chimaerostrobus minutus</u> wasn't just a new species, it also represented a new genus, or whole species group, and a missing piece in the evolution of trees.

JOSÉ O'GORMAN AND THE ANTARCTICAN MARINE REPTILES

Fossils of an ancient reptile called an elasmosaur were first spotted during a 1989 expedition. It took another 23 years before José O'Gorman, from the Argentina Antarctic Institute, was able to excavate them from the frozen soil of Seymour Island. Battling cold, snowy conditions that slowed down their work and held up plans to helicopter their fossils to Argentina's Marambio Base, O'Gorman's team unearthed the remains of the elasmosaur. These aquatic reptiles lived near the end of the Cretaceous period, 66 million years ago. At 11.8–14.8 tons (10.7–13.4 tonnes), O'Gorman's specimen measured 40 feet (12 m) from nose to tail—a tail which it may have used as a whiplike weapon cracked at super-fast speeds.

THOMAS MÖRS AND A 40-MILLION-YEAR-OLD FROG

A 40-million-year-old fossil of a frog was found on Seymour Island, which is now so cold that it would kill a human. Paleontologist Thomas Mörs, from the Swedish Museum of Natural History in Stockholm, said the frog showed that 40 million years ago Antarctica was still warm enough to keep a cold-blooded frog—and maybe other amphibians and reptiles—croaking happily. How could that be? Especially when you think that "just" six million years after this frog's lifetime, Antarctica began to ice over and frog population numbers fell to zero. In geological time, that's a quick freeze— something the frog fossil discovery helped prove was possible.

THE THING

In 2011, when Chilean scientists found something that looked like a flattened football, 11 x 7 inches (28 x 18 cm), they tucked it away in a museum. They simply called it "the Thing." Nine years later the Thing was identified as a 68-million-year-old egg. Whose egg? It's quite possible it was from a mosasaur, a giant swimming reptile. Only one animal is known to have a bigger egg—the extinct Madagascan elephant bird.

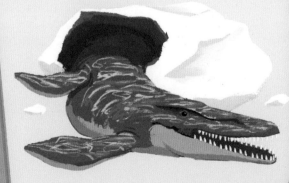

SOLVING THE MYSTERY OF AN ICY HISTORY

Scientists studying Antarctica often piece together clues from earlier eras by looking at the seafloor or the ice sheet. They do this by drilling into them like a straw into a milkshake. What comes up—known as a core—contains layers of material that have piled up year after year by either falling through the sea or from the sky and onto the ice. Like the rings on tree trunks, these layers show what conditions on Earth were like at the time they formed. Sediment cores pulled up from the seabed contain mud, sand, or rock that might have been dragged down by glaciers, fossils of creatures that lived long ago, and much more. Ice cores pulled up from glaciers contain frozen water and bubbles of air from centuries past. They can yield clues about the world when the ice formed: the sea temperature, the life of plankton at the surface or under the ice, how much sunlight shone through, and more.

JOHANN KLAGES AND THE ANCIENT RAINFOREST

Consider the bottom of the sea. Mud, sand, shells, and rocks form sediment as they fall or are washed there in layers over time. If you can pull them up in order, you can tell the time when they fell to the seafloor—geological time, that is—going back millions of years as you go through the layers. Johann Klages, from the Alfred Wegener Institute in Germany, and a team aboard the German ship <u>Polarstern</u>, drilled up a sediment core that looked like nothing special. But an X-ray revealed that it contained the root system of the kind of trees that only grow in a temperate rain forest, showing that Antarctica was once as warm as Europe is today.

YUZHEN YAN AND SOME VERY OLD AIR AND ICE

Antarctica's southern Allan Hills host a friendly competition between nations vying to find the oldest "blue" ice (freshwater glacial ice). In 2019, shards of 2.7-million-year-old ice found nearby yielded surprising news about the past. The ice is not buried as deep as you'd expect for something so old. Instead, it's found near a mountain range, where the deepest, oldest ice in the glacier is forced to the surface as the glacier slides over stone ridges below. Among the treasures found inside the ice core were meteorites and bubbles containing 1.5-million-year-old air. That air revealed a surprise: Yuzhen Yan, a Chinese paleoclimatologist at Princeton University, reported air bubbles containing surprisingly low levels of carbon dioxide despite the slightly higher temperatures during this period. This shows that the natural levels of carbon dioxide in the atmosphere haven't changed much over the past two million years. The rise we are seeing now, Yan says, is due to human activity.

DODGING ICEBERGS TO STUDY AT SEA

By now you've heard enough about stranded ships, shifting sea ice, and icebergs to know that doing research at sea in Antarctica can be perilous. In 2019, I joined scientists aboard the *JOIDES Resolution*, a ship that uses a huge drill to bring up sediment samples from the seafloor. We settled into berths (beds on a ship) for a two-month journey to the Amundsen Sea, into which both the Pine Island Glacier and the Thwaites Glacier flow—pushing icebergs right into our path.

During our expedition, ice watchers were working around the clock to keep us safe. They used satellite images and radar data to view the glacier as it broke up into the sea and keep track of passing icebergs, which were so big and dangerous that we couldn't allow them within a mile of the ship. Often the ship had to take evasive action, even in the midst of its important work of drilling up samples, as big icebergs seemed to aim themselves at our drill ship's massive steel hull, which was not built to stand up to even the littlest berg.

TWO TWEETING GLACIERS

Scientists have created Twitter profiles for the Pine Island and Thwaites glaciers, and often tweet jokey remarks about losing weight or scientists examining their bottoms. But findings here are no joke: the glaciers and adjoining ocean are heating up.

Pine Island Glacier
@AntarcticPIG — March 1

It seems many of you have been busy doing great science on me over the past few years and I have more than a few tabular icebergs worth of thanks to send around— stay tuned.

Also, sorry about that big one recently...

Thwaites Glacier
@ThwaitesGlacier — July 27

I'm just focusing on not falling apart.

We had hoped to sail near to the coast, but the amount of ice the glaciers shed kept us more than a hundred miles (160 km) out. Within a thousand miles (1,600 km) sailed two other research ships, both icebreakers—ships equipped to break a path through the ice. The Russian research vessel *Akademik Aleksandr Karpinskiy* was on its way to the Ross Sea, where it would use sound to analyze the sea floor. The U.S. icebreaker *Nathaniel B. Palmer* carried more scientists, who would work at the edge of the Thwaites Glacier as part of the International Thwaites Glacier Collaboration.

You can bet the Thwaites was a-twitter—it had never received so much attention. Teams of researchers camped atop of it, flew up over it, drilled down into it, sailed up to its edge, and sent gliders and submarines to dive beneath it. The scientists figured out how much sunlight the glacier reflects, gauged the health of the plankton on the underside of its ice sheet, and peeked at its grounding point— the place where its base scrapes the seafloor.

The warming ocean surges beneath the glacier, which has a hollow the size of Manhattan Island in New York City—a lot for a glacier a bit bigger than Florida.

Since snow and ice reflects sunlight back into the atmosphere, warming speeds up even more as they melt away. It's what's called a snowball effect, increasing as it rolls on. The collapse of the Thwaites Glacier alone could cause a worldwide sea level rise of more than half a meter (25 inches). And at that moment on the *JOIDES Resolution*, this huge cow of a glacier was calving right in front of us, the icebergs flowing out in the direction of our ship.

WALIUR RAHAMAN AND JI-HOON KIM DRILL INTO ANCIENT HISTORY

Aboard the JOIDES Resolution, scientists and science supporters from the Philippines, India, South Korea, China, Japan, Germany, France, the U.S., Canada, the U.K., Brazil, Norway, Sweden, and New Zealand worked to pull up the longest-ever sediment core from the Southern Ocean. Like the ice watchers, the scientists held round-the-clock positions in twos, each taking a 12-hour shift.

Waliur Rahaman from the National Centre for Antarctic and Ocean Research in India worked side by side with Ji-Hoon Kim of the Korea Institute of Geoscience and Mineral Resources to understand the chemistry of the mud and rock in the cores. Every other team analyzed their own aspect of the sediment core samples. Once the cruise was finished, they shared their samples with the world.

THE INTERNATIONAL THWAITES GLACIER COLLABORATION

The International Thwaites Glacier Collaboration (ITGC) is a special study mission, spread across five research seasons. It started in 2018 and is due to finish in 2023, even though it experienced delays because of the COVID-19 pandemic. This collaboration between the U.S.'s National Science Foundation and the U.K.'s National Environment Research Council (NERC) aims to examine the massive Thwaites Glacier from top to bottom, including the seafloor beneath it and the sea into which it flows—and has flowed for thousands of years. Now that it's moving faster as it thaws from within, and shedding icebergs like a dog sheds its winter coat, scientists are bringing a full toolbox to examine things closely.

Deep-diving Weddell and elephant seals also work for the ITGC. While scientists need to retrieve their ocean moorings, Autonomous Underwater Vehicles (robotic submarines), and gliders to get the data from them, satellite transmitter tags affixed to seals' heads send data each time the seals come up for breath.

A stable glacier's tongue licks out over the ocean to form a floating ice shelf that slows the descending river of ice.

The glacier goes faster or slower depending on its interaction with the "grounding line," the point where the glacier stops resting on the ground below and begins to float.

Warm currents

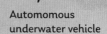

Automomous underwater vehicle

Scientists' work continues once they leave the field. Many scientists learn about Antarctica not by visiting, but by studying data. Much of the data gathered by the ITGC will become part of computer models, which demonstrate the conditions that the scientists in the field are seeing. The models allow scientists to tweak conditions and see the effects of the changes. This allows them to anticipate what might happen if, say, more warm water flows in under the glacier... and melts a bit more away.

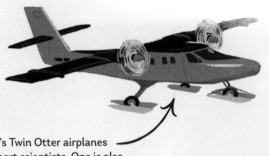

NERC's Twin Otter airplanes transport scientists. One is also fitted with radar instruments that measure the ice and the rock beneath it.

Snow falls and compacts at the head of a river of freshwater ice—the glacier.

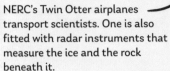

A team of scientists traverses the Thwaites Glacier from their camp. As they travel, they tow a radar sled that gives a more close and detailed scan of ice cracks and hardness, compared to the radar scan from the plane.

Scientists camp on the glacier to make observations and gather data. An array of seismometers is used to sense the depth of the seabed under the ice.

Ocean gliders can be deployed through holes drilled in the ice. They're used to examine the ocean water, including its temperature, density, saltiness, and pressure—factors that help researchers understand how the sea interacts with the ice. Video cameras and sonar (sound-emitting) devices also allow them to map the seafloor.

Gliders can only travel a few miles once they descend through their hole, so scientists also need seismic (sound) data taken from the glacier surface in order to build their map.

WEST ANTARCTIC ICE SHEET

THWAITES GLACIER

The Thwaites Glacier covers 74,000 square miles (192,000 square km)—bigger than Florida.

ANNA WÅHLIN AND THE UNDERWATER ROBOT

Autonomous underwater vehicles are put into the water from ships and can travel under the ice. Swedish scientist Anna Wåhlin deployed this HUGIN sub under Thwaites' ice shelf. It is named after a sea witch called Ran from Norse mythology.

SAILING THE SOUTHERN OCEAN

The Southern Ocean that surrounds Antarctica, like the rest of the world's oceans, is layered with channels of water with different temperatures and levels of salinity (saltiness). The rising and sinking of these layers, and the currents traveling through them, drives the ocean, sending every drop of water on a trip around the world. Scientists working on ships, in labs monitoring data sent by robots sailing the waves, or analyzing images and measurements taken from space are in a hurry to understand the Southern Ocean.

In 2019, three wind-powered surface-sailing robots called Saildrones—tall, sleek, and high-visibility orange—set off from South Africa, their bows set toward the Southern Ocean. Only one succeeded (the other two suffered storm damage and returned to port.) Saildrone 1020 became the first robot to sail all the way around Antarctica. Over 196 days, it traveled 13,670 miles (22,000 km), enduring 49-foot (15-m) waves, 80-mph (129-kmph) winds, and crashes with huge icebergs. Along with so many other research projects in Antarctica, its focus was to gather data where no ship or float could go. The Saildrone's data would aid scientists worldwide in understanding Antarctica's role in the balance of carbon dioxide in Earth's atmosphere and oceans. Collaborators from Japan to England, from Australia to California, eagerly awaited the Saildrone's data. It also collected information about weather and marine animals in the places it sailed.

ISABELLA ROSSO AND ALEJANDRO ORSI AND THE MIX OF THE SOUTHERN OCEAN

How do you dive into such a remote ocean? Robots can help there too! Italian scientists—Rosso from the Scripps Institution of Oceanography and Orsi from Texas A&M University—want to understand the mix of the Southern Ocean: what heat, salt, nutrients, and other ingredients are entering and exiting it, and how the layers of the sea stack up. If they could travel the ocean and take measurements from the surface and at multiple depth locations, they could figure out what's happening. But boarding a ship and covering the massive ocean surrounding Antarctica would be far too costly and risky.

Enter the SOCCOM (Southern Ocean Carbon and Climate Observations and Modeling) profiling float, a cylinder-shaped robot deployed from a ship that spends five years gathering the data that scientists need. The float dives down to take samples and measurements at different levels of the ocean, then bobs up to upload the data via satellite. This allows the scientists to analyze deep currents that carry water with different chemical make-ups and temperatures. Imagine a map created from the data transmitted from hundreds of SOCCOM floats all over the ocean. That map exists. Students can adopt and name the floats and use the map to trace the path of their school's own float, while tracking the data, too.

Studying the ice that floats on the ocean's surface along the coast also leads to new understanding of the continent it surrounds. Cores drilled into the ice shelf reveal a different cycle from those taken from the glacial ice of the ice sheet. They show the freeze and thaw of ice at the edges of the continent. When a team from the University of Bonn in Germany examined sea ice cores, they found evidence that, as the world warms, the Southern Ocean absorbs and stores more carbon, which means more food for organisms living there. They wonder: as fossil fuels continue to add carbon dioxide to Earth's atmosphere, what role will Antarctica's ocean play in helping balance carbon levels?

The answer isn't the ocean; it's what floats, swims, dives, and lives there. Antarctica's animals must adapt in response to changes in the menu. Does more food for some mean less for others? What impact will changes in temperature—and resulting changes in ice—have on them? To understand Antarctica, we've got to understand its food chain.

Chapter 3
WHAT LIVES HERE?

My job at Palmer Station was to help (and use my writing and art to tell the stories of) my team of scientists: Peter "Pete" Countway, Patricia "Paty" Matrai, and Carlton Rauschenberg, from the Bigelow Laboratory for Ocean Science in the U.S. This team was in Antarctica to track down invisible, microscopic beings in the rollicking sea off the Antarctic Peninsula. You might not realize it— I sure hadn't!—but plankton (algae, protozoa, microbes, and even the tiny animals) living at the surface of the sea play a big role in the way clouds are formed above it.

From our small inflatable boat lurching in waves that tossed up icy spray, I helped launch a rosette of tubes that would sink below the surface, then suck in water samples chock full of plankton. These microscopic floating plankton live near the shore at the edge of the ice. They hold secrets to how Antarctica changes and its future.

Like plants, some plankton photosynthesize sunlight to create food. This means they use the Sun's energy to transform simple materials into the food and energy they need. One type of plankton called *Phaeocystis* produces tiny airborne gases that get churned up and spewed higher by the waves. Some scientists call them plankton farts, others call them seeds for clouds. Water molecules stick onto these gassy "cloud seeds" and ride them high into the sky. This is what helps make Antarctica so cloudy—a phenomenon that impacts the weather patterns of the rest of the world, as clouds contribute to the cooling or warming of Earth's surface.

This all leads to Pete and Paty asking: As the ice retreats and Antarctica warms, what will happen to these clouds? And what will happen to the rest of the Antarctic food chain, the living things found there in surprising abundance?

ANTARCTIC FOOD CHAINS

Food chains show what eats what in a particular environment. This is just one example from the waters around Antarctica.

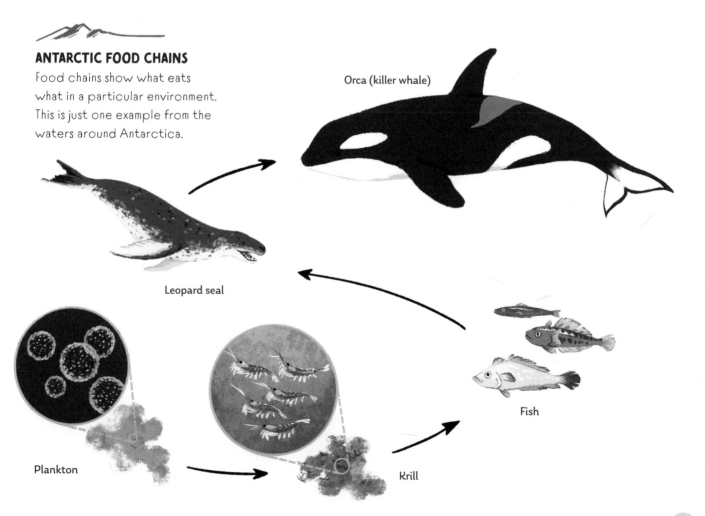

Orca (killer whale)

Leopard seal

Plankton

Krill

Fish

WEIRD ANTARCTIC WILDLIFE

THE ONLY BEARS IN ANTARCTICA

Tardigrades, nicknamed "water bears," are among the microbes that come to life after thawing from frozen Antarctic soil. Researcher Summer Xue said, "Every time we find a tardigrade, ... they look like they are dancing there and saying hi to you [from under the microscope]—and they make you feel happy."

Tardigrade

Antarctica is named for what it isn't: the Arctic. The name Arctic comes from the Greek word *arktos*, meaning "bear," and refers to the Great Bear constellation of stars that hangs over the north sky at night. Antarctic means the anti-Arctic—the far south—and there are no bears here, neither on the ice nor in the night sky.

You'd think nothing could thrive in Antarctica. It's the coldest, driest, and windiest continent in the world. The dinosaurs, trees, and frogs that thrived in Antarctica's forests, swamps, and warmer waters millions of years ago wouldn't last five minutes in today's Antarctic environment. But plenty of creatures do. Antarctic animals have changed radically from those warmth-wanting creatures to cold-comfortable ones. They've adapted their diets to what's available here, packed on fat to fight the freeze, and managed their migrations. Some have even made their own antifreeze or altered their cells or blood vessels. Among the goals for scientists is to understand what makes Antarctic ecosystems tick.

SUMMER XUE AND THE WORM FARM

Xia "Summer" Xue, from Zhengzhou, China, was among a team of scientists from Brigham Young University who dug up "ice cement" samples from the McMurdo Dry Valleys—the planet's coldest, driest, and windiest valleys. The bare ground there isn't really cement, but a rather rock-hard, frozen soil called permafrost, which, when it's thawed, comes to life with worms called nematodes. These tiny creatures have wet and dry modes. In the absence of water, nematodes shut down and dry like potato chips in a process called anhydrobiosis—a word that means they're alive, even in this dried-out state. After the nematodes had spent thousands of years like this, researchers watched as the flat dry organisms took water into their cells and came back to life.

Scientists want to know how long nematodes can survive, and what genes give them the ability to do so under such dry, cold conditions, as well as to create another survival tool: antifreeze chemicals that keep their cells from icing up.

Dry nematode

Wet nematode

Icefish blood

Angelfish blood

At two in the morning, in a pelting snowstorm, on a rough and rocking ocean I got up close with another of Antarctica's weird, wondrous creatures. Thomas Desvignes, a French researcher from the University of Oregon, knelt on the slimy deck of the U.S. research ship *Laurence M. Gould*, pawing through the catch just dumped from a big seine (a type of net). With gloved hands, he plucked out a dark-green fish and handed it to me. What an amazing moment!

Cradling the fish close to my chest, I carried it to a bubbling tank where it would join other fish set aside so Desvignes could study their unique adaptations. Icefish lack red blood cells, which all other vertebrates use to transport oxygen around their bodies. But icefish live without them, thanks to extra-wide blood vessels, a large heart, and antifreeze proteins. These keep their colorless, see-through blood from freezing, even at 29°F (-1.8°C)—a temperature that would freeze freshwater and red blood in marine fish anywhere else on Earth. (Other Antarctic fish have this antifreeze, too.) Icefish lack scales, and Desvignes thinks they may even breathe through their skin. But all these adaptations leave icefish vulnerable to warming waters.

A LOT AND ALONE
Most life in Antarctica is found in or close by to the sea, but there are some land animals to be found here.

Antarctica's only terrestrial bird is the snowy sheathbill.

Antarctica's most abundant land, or terrestrial, animals are nematode worms.

Antarctica's only terrestrial insect is *Belgica antarctica*, or the Antarctic midge. It is also the largest solely terrestrial animal in Antarctica.

WHAT'S EVERYBODY EATING?

Sure, Antarctica could easily kill even the most warmly dressed human, but it's just right for its native animals. Among them are some fine examples of a puzzling phenomenon called polar gigantism. Although scientists are not exactly sure why, many species living in the far north or south are the biggest of their kind. Take krill, the foundation of the Antarctic food chain, eaten by just about every animal—fish, seals, penguins, and whales. A krill is a little pinkish-reddish-brownish creature similar to a crab or a prawn, known as a crustacean. Antarctic krill grow to around the length of a paper clip, which is about twice as big as krill elsewhere on Earth.

Billions of tons of krill live in the Southern Ocean, sucking up the quadrillions of tiny phytoplankton that photosynthesize at the sea surface, turning light to food the way plants do. Krill also consume ice algae that dwell on the bottom of sea ice, and form such massive swarms that cameras on satellites orbiting Earth can capture clouds of them coloring the sea. Organs on their sides called photophores send out flashes of light as signals, also a mystery to scientists.

At 2.3 inches (6 cm), krill in Antarctica are twice as big as krill elsewhere on Earth.

Octopus

Deep-sea sponges may reach over 6 feet (1.8 m) in size.

Icefish

Sea spiders, typically 0.39 inch (1 cm) long in warmer seas, may approach almost 14 inches (40 cm) in length.

Jellyfish tentacles
may extend as long
as 12 feet (3.6 m).

A colossal squid was captured
by fishermen seeking
Antarctic toothfish in the
Ross Sea. This one weighed
more than half a ton (470 kg),
making it the heaviest-known
colossal squid.

ANTARCTIC GIANTS

Polar gigantism is weird because it exists
in lots of unrelated taxa, or species
groups, while other Antarctic species
are of similar sizes to their warmer-
dwelling cousins. Some of the giant-sized
animals of Antarctica are shown here.

CHUCK AND MAGGIE AMSLER AND THE ANTARCTIC UNDERSEA FOREST

Deep down where the krill spend their days, the dark hides an amazing environment only ever seen by a handful of humans. Sure, the forests that once covered this continent in trees are long gone. But there's another forest—an underwater forest that biologist Charles "Chuck" Amsler says is the most exciting part of Antarctica. He's spent his life scuba diving (with more than 1,000 dives in Antarctica alone) to research the seaweed living in the unique environment at the bottom of the Southern Ocean. His team studies the chemicals that seaweed produces to defend itself against predators. Among those diving with Chuck is his wife Margaret "Maggie" Amsler, a krill researcher who took a submersible vehicle nearly 3,284 feet (1,000 m) deep into a cloud of krill in search of the colossal squid. Scientists were pretty sure it was down there, even though no one had even ever seen one in its natural habitat until 2021—just on a fishing line!

It's been decades since the Amslers, from the University of Alabama at Birmingham, began working at Palmer Station. Recently they received an honor they're not especially pleased about: an island off the coast was named after them. What's so bad about that? Well, when the Amslers first arrived there, the island was buried under the shelf of the Marr Ice Piedmont, part of a massive glacier. Over the time they've been working there, the area has warmed so much that the ice shelf slipped into the sea, revealing the island below. New islands continue to emerge in Antarctica as temperatures increase and the glaciers thaw and recede.

Sure, Antarctic krill are big. But their numbers have dropped 80 percent in the last 50 years. This is in part because global warming has thawed sea ice, reducing the ice algae food supply that they rely on, but also due to overfishing of krill in Antarctica (krill is used to feed livestock and pets, and also to raise fish.)

LUIS HÜCKSTÄDT AND THE KRILL MAP

Krill is an essential food for so many Antarctic animals: penguins, whales (the biggest consumers of krill), and undersea locals such as seastars, those weird, clear-blooded icefish, and perhaps—just perhaps!—the elusive colossal squid all eat krill. Crabeater seals feed on krill too, despite the name given them by explorers who misread the contents of their stomachs as crab, not krill. It's only when they're hunting for krill that crabeater seals dive. In a new study, Chilean scientist Luis Hückstädt from the University of California Santa Cruz has been using satellite tracker tags (like the ones the ITGC uses with elephant seals) to detect when the crabeater seals dive, and using this data to map krill.

One solution involves turning Antarctic waters into a massive sanctuary. The continued loss of krill impacts animals that depend on krill as part of their diets. Apart from helping out Antarctic species that eat krill, any decisions to protect them could also help reduce climate change. That's because they migrate daily from the sea surface, where they eat, to the deep sea. Down in the depths they expel carbon dioxide, effectively removing this greenhouse gas from the air and storing it underwater.

Who wants krill, anyway?

Penguins. Penguins in multitudes. Penguins who arrive out of nowhere in flocks that fling themselves along the sea surface, flippers flashing like wings, arcing in and out of the water the way dolphins do. Penguins who throw themselves, scrabbling, onto ice ledges, where they stop being sleek and commence being comical. Penguins who waddle or belly-flop, feed their silly fluffy giant chicks, or just stare with wise eyes.

THESE ARE THE PENGUINS YOU ARE LOOKING FOR

Ask any Antarctic researcher what penguins are really like and they might mention the graceful goofiness, the squawking, the cruel attacks on their chicks by big birds called skua, the bloody spots left on the ice after a leopard seal has paid a visit, or the lunges of orca trying to skim penguin lunch off the ice floes. They might mention one of these things. But they will absolutely mention the penguins' odor: unimaginable and unforgettable. The smell comes from their waste: a smoky, stinky combination of ammonia (a chemical with a strong smell like cat pee) and rotten fish. To be precise, it's the penguins' chief diet of krill—after it's gone through the penguins.

You don't have to do special analysis to see that climate change is impacting Antarctica. Just watch the penguins. Notice which ones wind up where each winter and which ones show up seasonally the next summer. Over recent years this has been changing, as penguins respond to retreating sea ice and go where they must to find the ice they need to live and breed on.

Take emperor penguins, for example—the tallest, most elegant penguins. They need sea ice that is thick and stable enough to raise chicks, but not so far from water that they can't find food or have to walk too far to get to it.

OBSERVE THE PENGUIN

Adélie. Gentoo. Emperor. Chinstrap. These four penguin species are truly at home in Antarctica. Three other species migrate in and out of Antarctica: king, macaroni and rockhopper penguins.

DO NOT PICK UP A PENGUIN

Scientists receive carefully issued permits to measure and test wildlife.

Emperor penguin

Chinstrap penguin

Adélie penguin

King penguin

STÉPHANIE JENOUVRIER AND THE EMPEROR PENGUIN

Stéphanie Jenouvrier, a French seabird ecologist working at Woods Hole Oceanographic Institution in Massachusetts, projected scenarios for emperor penguins. These are possible situations they could encounter depending on how quickly the climate warms: What if...

◆ the global temperature rises by 2.7°F (1.5°C) by 2100? This is the goal of the Paris Agreement, adopted in 2015 by nearly all nations, to put a lid on climate change. In this best-case scenario, 31% of emperor penguins could perish.

◆ the temperature rises by 3.6°F (2°C) by 2100? 44% of emperor penguins could perish.

◆ the temperature rises by 5.4°–9°F (3–5°C) by 2100? This is the situation projected to happen if the world doesn't rein in its current trend of greenhouse gas emissions. In this worst-case scenario, 98% of emperor penguins could be doomed. So the number of penguins that survives depends on whether people can slow or stop climate change.

Certain penguin species may handle climate change better than others. Gentoo penguins, for example, are increasing in number on the Antarctic Peninsula, replacing the Adélies that used to thrive on the sea ice there. Why? Because the Antarctic Peninsula is warming so fast. Winter temperatures there have risen by 7.2°C (12°F) over the last 65 years. In recent years, Adélie penguins have migrated further south to nest, following the ice, leaving more food for the gentoos. Gentoo penguins may succeed better in other areas too because of their food preferences. They'll switch up their meals depending on what's available—fish, squid, or krill—while other penguins, such as chinstraps, that insist on eating only krill could decline along with their prey.

WHO AGREED?

In 2018, the Intergovernmental Panel on Climate Change reported on the need to limit global warming to just 1.5°C (2.7°F) more than the start of the industrial age. The Paris Agreement was signed by 195 nations in support of this goal.

Rockhopper penguin

Gentoo penguin

Macaroni penguin

SEALS AND WHALES

Among the six seal species native to Antarctica—Ross, Weddell, elephant, fur, leopard, and crabeater seals—elephant seals are the most massive: the gigantic "beachmasters" may exceed 8,800 pounds (4,000 kg). Like the rest of the seals, layers of fur and blubber keep them insulated against cold Antarctic air. Elephant seals' ability to stay underwater for as long as two hours and to dive up to 1.2 miles (2 km) helps them keep those big bodies fed. Seals have an extra-silvery backing to the retinas in their eyes that lets them absorb more light in deep, dark water. And sonar, the ability to echolocate by making sounds that bounce off solid objects, may assist them in finding their prey of fish, squid, and krill.

Elephant seal

PREM GILL AND THE FARAWAY SEALS

Prem Gill, who works for Cambridge University's (U.K.) Scott Polar Research Institute, wanted to know what would happen to seals living on the sea ice as conditions change. But the seals' hangouts were so far from stations that they couldn't be accessed by boat or plane, never mind on foot. Gill put special cameras into play; they use heat, color, and light to count the seals on the ground. He coordinated them with data from very high-quality sensors on satellites. Capable of spotting a laptop, a book, or a baby seal that's lying on the ice from Earth's orbit, these sensors allow Gill to count seals and assess the conditions of the ice they prefer.

He wants to anticipate the decisions seals will make as the sea ice changes, where they will go, and how they will be affected.

Satellite transmitter tags like Gill's have helped other scientists ask and answer key questions about Antarctica. It's hard for scientists to get to Antarctica, challenging to dive for longer than half an hour in the below-freezing temperature waters, and expensive and difficult to deploy submersibles, and robotic probes. The seals offer another way to study the waters.

Sei whale

You might think no predator would take on elephant seals, but orca have been known to. Orca, the "killer" toothed whales, will also prey on other seals, including the vicious leopard seal, as well as penguins.

Like penguins, elephant seals coat the territory they colonize with their excrement. Some scientists travel to Antarctica in search of this poop. They have found that penguin and seal poop serve an important purpose in Antarctica: to transfer nutrients from the sea to the land, and not just coastal land. The ammonia in the poop hits the air, which carries it up to several miles inland, where it enters the soil to provide nutrients to mosses, lichens, and tiny animals such as mites. Understanding elephant seal poop has helped to assess the Antarctic environment so it can be understood even as it undergoes change. It's also shown that an elephant seal or penguin colony can impact land 240 times its area.

The six species of baleen whale (blue, fin, humpback, sei, minke, and southern right whales) commonly found in these waters gulp krill by the ton, sieving the sea through their comblike baleen. Using helicopters and drones, or just looking out from the decks of stations or ships, scientists spy pods of humpbacks "bubble net feeding": circling schools of krill to gather them in nets of bubbles before lunging through to inhale food-filled water.

STALKED BY A LEOPARD SEAL

As I walked on the wharf at Palmer Station, a friend called out from a window above and made the scuba diver's sign of a letter L with her thumb and pointer finger: leopard seal! I turned in time to catch sight of the tail flipper of the seal below me in the inlet. "Come back!" I called. Shockingly, it did. A leopard seal, green-gray, dark-speckled, stony-eyed, gazing up at me with the look of a diner considering the menu: was I edible? Automatically, maybe instinctively, I did the quick calculation of the prey: How far down from the wharf was the water? How far from the water could the seal leap? Could I escape in time? "Go away!" I said now. Luckily it did.

Leopard seal

RULES OF ENGAGEMENT

Regulations under the Antarctic Treaty restrict interactions with Antarctic animals. The simple rule of thumb is: if the animal changes its behavior because of you, you're too close.

Arnoux's beaked whales migrate from deep Antarctic waters to continental shelf areas covered in pack ice, such as the Ross Sea.

GIANT ANIMALS OF ANTARCTICA

SEABIRDS

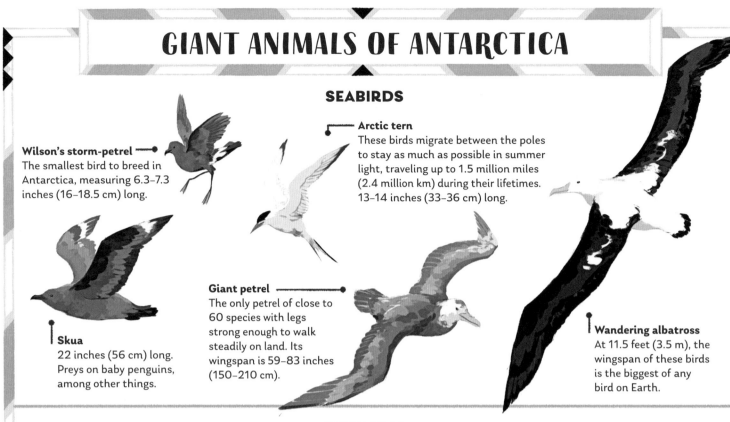

Wilson's storm-petrel
The smallest bird to breed in Antarctica, measuring 6.3–7.3 inches (16–18.5 cm) long.

Arctic tern
These birds migrate between the poles to stay as much as possible in summer light, traveling up to 1.5 million miles (2.4 million km) during their lifetimes. 13–14 inches (33–36 cm) long.

Skua
22 inches (56 cm) long. Preys on baby penguins, among other things.

Giant petrel
The only petrel of close to 60 species with legs strong enough to walk steadily on land. Its wingspan is 59–83 inches (150–210 cm).

Wandering albatross
At 11.5 feet (3.5 m), the wingspan of these birds is the biggest of any bird on Earth.

PENGUINS

There are 18 species of penguin worldwide, but only 7 live in Antarctica.

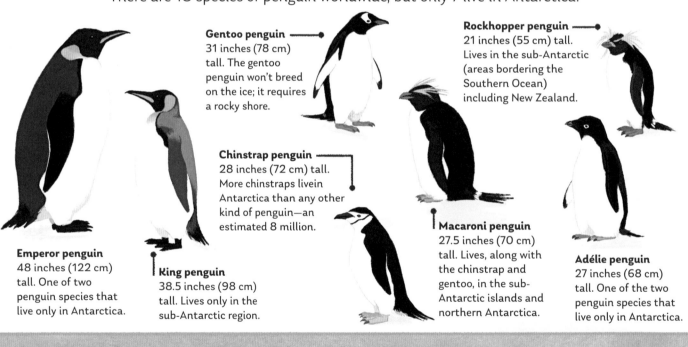

Gentoo penguin
31 inches (78 cm) tall. The gentoo penguin won't breed on the ice; it requires a rocky shore.

Rockhopper penguin
21 inches (55 cm) tall. Lives in the sub-Antarctic (areas bordering the Southern Ocean) including New Zealand.

Chinstrap penguin
28 inches (72 cm) tall. More chinstraps livein Antarctica than any other kind of penguin—an estimated 8 million.

Emperor penguin
48 inches (122 cm) tall. One of two penguin species that live only in Antarctica.

King penguin
38.5 inches (98 cm) tall. Lives only in the sub-Antarctic region.

Macaroni penguin
27.5 inches (70 cm) tall. Lives, along with the chinstrap and gentoo, in the sub-Antarctic islands and northern Antarctica.

Adélie penguin
27 inches (68 cm) tall. One of the two penguin species that live only in Antarctica.

THE ELUSIVE COLOSSAL SQUID

Estimated at 46 feet (14 m) and weighing up to 1,100 pounds (500 kg)—guesswork is involved, since a completely intact adult colossal squid has not yet been found.

WHALES

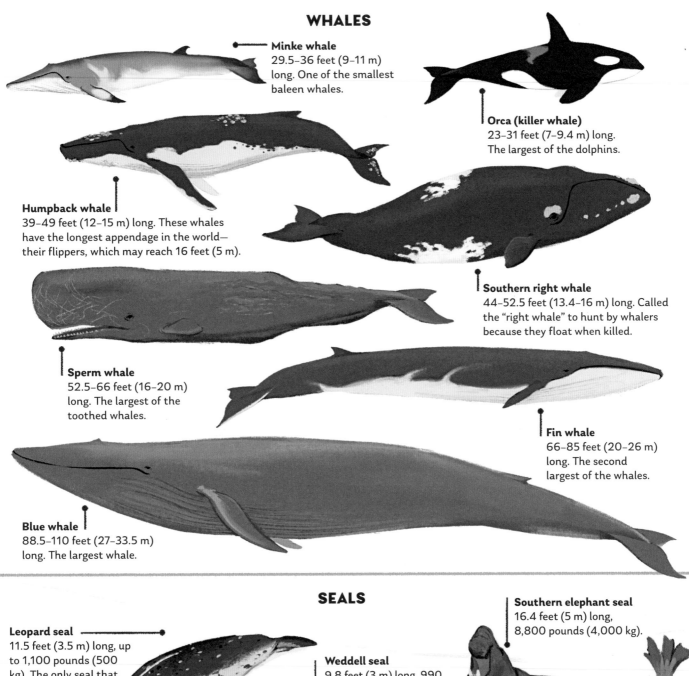

Minke whale
29.5–36 feet (9–11 m) long. One of the smallest baleen whales.

Orca (killer whale)
23–31 feet (7–9.4 m) long. The largest of the dolphins.

Humpback whale
39–49 feet (12–15 m) long. These whales have the longest appendage in the world—their flippers, which may reach 16 feet (5 m).

Southern right whale
44–52.5 feet (13.4–16 m) long. Called the "right whale" to hunt by whalers because they float when killed.

Sperm whale
52.5–66 feet (16–20 m) long. The largest of the toothed whales.

Fin whale
66–85 feet (20–26 m) long. The second largest of the whales.

Blue whale
88.5–110 feet (27–33.5 m) long. The largest whale.

SEALS

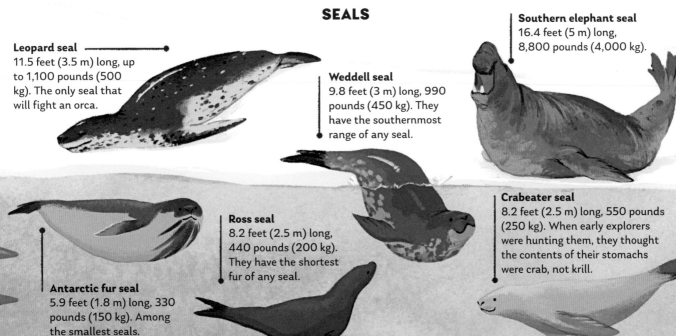

Leopard seal
11.5 feet (3.5 m) long, up to 1,100 pounds (500 kg). The only seal that will fight an orca.

Weddell seal
9.8 feet (3 m) long, 990 pounds (450 kg). They have the southernmost range of any seal.

Southern elephant seal
16.4 feet (5 m) long, 8,800 pounds (4,000 kg).

Crabeater seal
8.2 feet (2.5 m) long, 550 pounds (250 kg). When early explorers were hunting them, they thought the contents of their stomachs were crab, not krill.

Ross seal
8.2 feet (2.5 m) long, 440 pounds (200 kg). They have the shortest fur of any seal.

Antarctic fur seal
5.9 feet (1.8 m) long, 330 pounds (150 kg). Among the smallest seals.

LIFE ON OTHER WORLDS?

Besides its massive glaciers and oceanic coastline, Antarctica is a land of over 400 lakes, although each of them is hidden beneath miles of glacial ice. Lake Vostok, the largest, lies under 13,100 feet (4,000 m) of glacial ice. Russia's Vostok Station sits right on top of it. At 5,800 square miles (15,000 square km) in area, it's the world's 16th-largest lake, but nobody has ever seen it.

In 1996, measurements made from satellites gave scientists the information they needed to prove Lake Vostok existed. Scientists estimate that it was sealed off by ice some 15 million years ago. The water in the lake stays liquid below normal freezing temperatures because of the pressure of so much ice on top of it and plays host to thousands of organisms. Lake Vostok research suggests that similar life-forms could live in the ice-covered oceans on Jupiter's moon Europa, Saturn's moon Enceladus, and other cold celestial bodies.

RECORD FOR RESEARCH
On July 21, 1983, Vostok Station experienced the coldest naturally occurring temperature ever recorded on Earth: -128.6° F (-89.2° C).

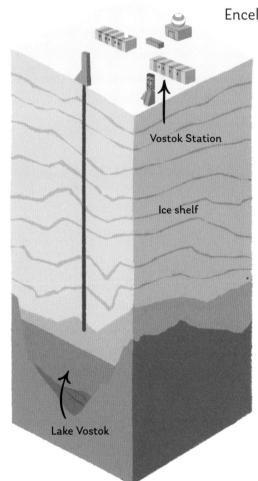

Vostok Station

Ice shelf

Lake Vostok

Lake Mercer, 373 miles (600 km) from the South Pole, is another lake hidden far below the surface of a glacier. In 2019, a team of scientists called SALSA (Subglacial Antarctic Lakes Scientific Access) pressed a hot-water drill 0.6 miles (1 km) deep into the lake and brought up samples. Once they had been thawed, scientists could study the microbes in the sample—each smaller than the point of a pin—including crustaceans (creatures such as crabs and shrimp) and tardigrades (also known as water bears). These life-forms offer clues to warm phases in Antarctic history—including those that took place as recently as the last 10,000 years or as long ago as 120,000 years. The tiny creatures might have been washed here by waters flowing down from the Transantarctic Mountains or they could have been scraped off the bottom of a glacier sliding by long ago.

NON-NATIVE LIFE

Humans are newcomers to Antarctica and have few potential predators apart from leopard seals (if you happen to be diving), elephant seals (if you get in their way), and orca (you never know). To aid in their own transportation and food supply people have imported ponies, dogs, cats, cows, pigs, and (by accident) perhaps the odd rat, spider, or mite. Since the 1960s, non-native species other than humans have been phased out in order to keep the Antarctic environment intact.

In 1994, the last sled dogs in Antarctica left Britain's Rothera Station, leaving the continent harsher and less fuzzy. Now Antarctic research would rely on human ingenuity alone. As the last dog team mushed toward the ship that would take them back north, they passed Hägglunds, train-engine-sized tractors with giant snow treads carrying people and cargo, among the snow machines of the future.

Apart from the nematode worms and frozen water bears, life barely exists in the middle of Antarctica, except in human form. No animals but us humans have an interest in the South Pole, the katabatic winds (which sweep viciously from the Transantarctic Mountains), or the wind-whipped ice waves called sastrugi that criss-cross the glaciers.

Chapter 4
THE HUMAN CITIZENS OF ANTARCTICA

There's no bridge to Antarctica, no road or train line. The only way to get there is by air or sea. First, fly to a port near Antarctica—"near" meaning hundreds of miles away: the Falkland Islands (part of the U.K., off the coast of Argentina); Christchurch, New Zealand; Punta Arenas, Chile; Hobart, Australia; Ushuaia, Argentina; or other smaller ports.

Now check in with your expedition and pick up your extreme cold weather (ECW) gear: layers of clothes, face-covering balaclavas, neckwarmers that make you look like a turtle, and boots that look like bunny feet. Antarctic arrivals add ECW gear to underlayers (from long underwear on up) brought from home.

Next, prepare the gear you've packed for your work. Research station workers and scientists bring everything from sleds to submarines to ingredients for sourdough bread, drones to GoPros to weather balloons, journals, laptops, family photos, vials for samples, and even violins. In addition to the above—well, apart from the violin, I don't play the violin—I brought fairy lights, art supplies, and a red wool blanket that has traveled with me from the Arctic to the Antarctic and many other places in between.

PANDEMIC POSTPONEMENT

In 2020–21, when COVID-19 caused a global pandemic, the most important job was preventing the virus from reaching Antarctica. Winter teams arriving for the 2020–21 season quarantined for weeks aboard ships or in ports before boarding planes. Once the teams were cleared and got settled at the stations, the cargo planes were grounded. Personnel at the stations were limited to those required to keep the stations running, and to those maintaining ongoing experiments. As a result, much research was cut off for several seasons.

At last, board your transport to Antarctica, most likely a cargo plane or a ship reinforced to withstand the ice. Don't expect to take off or ship out on time; delays can come from weather, ice state, cargo delivery, equipment issues, and more. Plenty of Ice Flights "boomerang"—turn back when conditions get worse on the journey.

FLYING IN?

McMurdo Station's (U.S.) runway, Phoenix Airfield, handles the massive C-17 cargo planes and ski-equipped LC-130 crafts capable of carrying thousands of pounds of cargo and people. From McMurdo, you can go on to the Amundsen-Scott South Pole Station, the Dry Valleys, and other inland stations and camps.

Thirty more research stations, representing 16 nations, have aircraft facilities, but they might not look like any airport you've ever seen. Don't expect tarmac! Most aircraft land and take off on runways built on gravel, sea ice, blue ice (freshwater ice) or snow. Some are equipped to handle only fixed-wing aircraft with skis, while others only have helipads. Among the stations with planes or helicopters, few can handle aircraft capable of transporting personnel on and off the continent. So, while you might be able to use their runways, your destinations are limited by the distance you can fly and return on a single tank of fuel.

COMING BY SHIP?

Punta Arenas, Chile, is the main port for ships bound for the Antarctic Peninsula or the West Antarctic Ice Sheet, including hot research spots in the Amundsen Sea such as the Pine Island and Thwaites glaciers; Queen Maud Land with its active volcanoes; and research stations such as Argentina's San Martín on the Antarctic Peninsula, which is out of helicopter range of South America. Brace yourself for a stormy crossing through the Drake Passage, where the waves exceed 28 feet (8.5 m), coming in intervals as short as 13 seconds apart, in ships that can't go more than 10 or 11 miles per hour (16–18 km/h).

ANTARCTIC AUTOS

The first car on the continent, an Arrol-Johnston, came to Antarctica with Ernest Shackleton's Nimrod Expedition, which attempted to reach the South Pole from 1907 to 1909.

Australia's Mawson Station was the first to try using everyday cars for transport in Antarctica. They brought Volkswagen Beetles to the continent for driving on hard-packed snow or ice. Normal tires don't work on deep, soft snow, so these days vehicles with belts, such as tractors, or skids, like snowmobiles, are preferred.

Volkswagen Beetle

Sno-Cat tractor

WHERE TO STAY

It's among the highlights of a scientist's career to come to Antarctica for research. The continent is dotted with close to 40 year-round research facilities representing about 20 nations, with additional countries maintaining summer-only stations. About 1,000 humans populate Antarctica in winter, jumping to 10,000 in summer.

The research stations are like small cities where everyone plays a part, and the field camps and research ships are like small towns—every person is vital. Hundreds of scientists come from around the world, as well as support crews who run the research stations. Keeping the lights on, providing food, and managing shelter, transportation, waste, and scientific operations means the stations need kitchen staff, carpenters, managers, engineers, navigators, ice watchers, electricians, doctors, drivers, mountaineers (to teach snow and ice safety procedures), and technicians prepared to help researchers set up field sites or to trouble-shoot issues with vehicles, instruments, or procedures. Storytellers of all stripes are needed there, too, including dancers, musicians, writers, artists, comic creators, reporters, playwrights, and puppeteers.

A TALENT FOR FUN

When Ernest Shackleton hired his crew for one of the first Antarctica expeditions, he paid attention to their skills, but also to their talents. Musicians, artists, photographers, filmmakers, and more were welcome, not only for their ability to tell his story, but also for their ability to improve the quality of life during the expedition.

At every Antarctic station, talent shows, concerts, parties, karaoke, and other fun activities are as vital for morale as great food. If you go, pack your penguin costume, your guitar, your kazoo, and your sense of humor. They won't go to waste.

Step outside in the deep-freeze of Antarctica and fling a cup of water over your head. Instant snow!

WHAT IS A RESEARCH STATION?

Scott Base, sometimes known as the Kiwi Station, maintains the New Zealand scientific presence in Antarctica. Named for the British Navy Captain Robert Falcon Scott, who led two expeditions to Antarctica, Scott Base was built to support the Commonwealth Trans-Antarctic Expedition, and opened in 1957. Hut Point is the site of the only building left from Scott's expedition. The other buildings, built at least 23 feet (7 m) apart for fire safety, are all connected by enclosed passageways, eliminating the need to suit up and face the elements when going, say, from dorm to dinner, or dinner to the lab. They are all painted a shade of green called Chelsea Cucumber. Scott Base is located below Mount Erebus, 33 feet (10 m) above the sea ice, and just a few miles from the 1,200-person McMurdo Station (U.S.), with its two airfields that accommodate LC-130 transport planes flying in from Christchurch, New Zealand,

CHANGING STATIONS

Stations change with the needs of their nations and researchers, and sometimes for political reasons too. Vernadsky Station belonged to the U.K. (as Faraday Station) until 1996. Faraday Station had started in 1935 with a small cabin and was steadily improved until the British government opted to transfer ownership to another nation: Ukraine.

bearing passengers and cargo. McMurdo Station and Scott Base serve as jumping-off points for the McMurdo Dry Valleys, Amundsen-Scott South Pole Station, and other stations and field sites. In its early days, the base was home to sled dogs, which helped with transport out into the field before they were banned in 1986. Scott Base also hosts science scuba divers. The station sees 300 people staying for summer stints, but the winter population drops to a dozen or so.

AURORA AUSTRALIS

Imagine a sky that appears draped with an iridescent, shimmering curtain of green light—with sudden bursts of every color in the rainbow. That's the aurora, a phenomenon that happens in the far north (where it's called the aurora borealis, or northern lights) and far south (where it's called the aurora australis, or southern lights). A magical experience for those who see it, the aurora is the product of a combination of magnetic forces from both the Sun and Earth.

Scott Base plan

1 Hatherton laboratory

2 Living space and library

3 Laundry

4 Living space and medical room

5 Kitchens, mess hall, and recreation room

6 Power plant and water treatment facilities

7 Communications equipment rooms and offices

8 Workshops

9 Laboratory, gym, and cargo warehouse

MELINDA ODUM AND THE ROTHERA STATION WHARF

Melinda Odum is an engineer who worked on the team for the British Antarctic Survey that designed a new wharf, a landing place for ships coming to Rothera, a British research station on the Antarctic Peninsula. She specializes in building structures in coastal environments. Rothera's new wharf will be capable of docking large research vessels such as the new polar research ship for Great Britain, the RRS Sir David Attenborough, and will make scientific studies involving small boats easier.

OKSANA SAVENKO WATCHES FOR WHALES

The first time marine biologist Oksana Savenko, from the National Antarctic Scientific Centre of Ukraine, went to Vernadsky Station for a few weeks in 2018, she gathered water, plankton, and seaweed—different biological samples for other scientists—and fitted her own work in between.

The next year, she wintered over—the first woman to do so in 22 years. Before then, the male scientists had mostly prohibited women from working at the station, making up excuses about why women shouldn't join them. They said that women would break the equipment and weren't strong enough for the tough jobs. Now Oksana was back for a 15-month stay to continue a long-term study of Antarctic cetaceans (whales, dolphins, and porpoises)—too important to delay. Not only would she observe, identify, count, and study the health and behaviour of orca and humpback, Antarctic minke, the rarer southern right, and Arnoux's beaked whales, she also assessed the conditions and life in the waters they were swimming in. Oksana intends to return to Vernadsky to continue this study.

KRIS PERRY AND WASTE IN ANTARCTICA

I visited Kris Perry in his office at Palmer Station—a TARDIS (Dr. Who's blue phone box and time machine) built at the top of a hill. Kris, who first came to Antarctica as a kitchen worker, now works in waste management at Palmer Station. He oversees the sorting, recycling, packing, and shipping of waste. Special attention is paid to spills of any kind and most station visitors learn how to clean up spills so that nothing is added to the environment. Recycling has to be sorted and shipped to Chile, as does other solid waste destined for a landfill. A few food scraps, such as chicken bones and avocado pits, are burned in Palmer Station's incinerator. Hazardous waste, such as used fuel or toxic or radioactive laboratory waste, is sent to McMurdo Station. The ship that resupplies McMurdo Station each year returns to the U.S. with its cargo of waste from all three U.S. stations, and it is processed there.

TOURING ANTARCTICA

Every summer, in addition to scientists and their support crews, thousands of tourists arrive on the Antarctic Peninsula in small cruise ships, generally from Argentina or New Zealand. Would you like to see Antarctica? You're not alone. Antarctic tourism began with ship trips in the 1950s, plane flyovers in the 1970s, and now cruises featuring visits to research stations, hikes on glaciers, and even kayaking among penguin-dotted islands.

According to the International Association of Antarctic Tour Operators, 56,000 people visited Antarctica in the 2018–19 season. New rules for cruise ships were put in place in 2017 in order to reduce the possibility of accidents involving oil spills, and to prevent damage to frequently visited sites. Concerns include impacts on animals (at one place, elephant seals disturbed by tourists have fallen from cliffs) and the possibility that seeds or other invasive species could be carried into Antarctica on people's clothing.

THE LATEST IN STATIONS

Ormond House, established by the Scottish National Antarctic Expedition in 1903, became the first permanent base in Antarctica. It was later sold to Argentina. New stations are still being founded. Jang Bogo Station was opened in 2014 by the South Korean Antarctic program in Terra Nova ("new land") Bay.

Signpost at
Vernadsky Station

THE STATION THAT SKIS

An historic list of Antarctic research stations includes the categories CLOSED and ACTIVE. The CLOSED stations cite reasons including glaciology (ice) and meteorology (weather), while others are simply "lost."

That brings me to Halley Research Station, a U.K. station that can ski to get to safer ice. The first Halley Station went up in 1956. Over the years, so much snow fell on its site, on the Brunt Ice Shelf in the southeast Weddell Sea, that the first four stations built there were buried and crushed. Their remains would drift with the ice. When they reached the edge of the shelf, they'd be lost to sea.

THE HOLE ABOVE HALLEY

Halley Station scientists have studied the ozone layer of Earth's atmosphere since 1956. The ozone layer, a natural sunscreen against the Sun's radiation, thinned because of manmade compounds in the air. In 1985, researchers there were the first to identify the hole in the ozone layer, leading to an international decision to reduce use of the troublesome chemicals, which has improved conditions.

Halley V—the fifth Halley Station—opened its doors in 1989. This station wouldn't get buried in snow! It had legs that could be jacked up to elevate it above the snow drifts and let the snow blow under it and away. When Halley V closed, it was dismantled and taken out of Antarctica to make room for 2012's Halley VI, the world's first relocatable research facility. This latest station is not only jacked up, but movable, too—vital, since the movement of the ice shelf can create dangerous gaps and chasms. Halley VI's hydraulic legs don't only lengthen, they ride on skis. This allows the entire station to ski-daddle off to a safer location on the 427-foot-(130-m-)thick ice shelf, with heavy tractor machines towing it away from trouble to more solid ice.

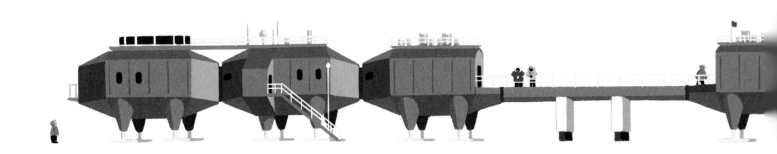

The Halley VI station is built out of eight modules, called pods. The big red pod in the center contains communal areas and a dining space, while the blue pods hold dorms and labs. Each pod can be raised or moved separately or they can form a train and ski off. During the 2017–18 season, the station skied 14 miles (23 km) away from a chasm that had opened in the ice. A network of seven GPS sensors monitors the continuous changes in the ice and alerts people on the station when a move needs to be considered.

OUT OF THIS WORLD ENVIRONMENTS

Some say space is the final frontier, but parts of Antarctica can seem just as remote. For example, the ridges of the Transantarctic Mountains are a tough destination and camp site. But if you're a scientist who wants to bring home samples from a long way off, you can't beat it. These wilds hold treasure—rocks and shards that have whizzed to Earth from space, hot trails streaming behind them, and dropped, sizzling, onto untouched Antarctic ice. The forces of glacier, mountain, wind, and weather cause meteorites to accumulate there, so from time to time the Antarctic Search for Meteorites Program (ANSMET) sets up camp and scours the terrain for space rocks. ANSMET is part of Case Western Reserve University in Ohio. These rockhounds have gathered more than 20,000 meteorite samples, which are sent to researchers around the world so they can discover not only the history of Antarctica, but the history of our solar system.

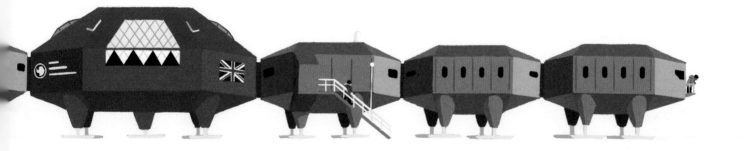

READY FOR ANYTHING

Among the first things visitors do when they reach this harsh continent is learn a few tricks of the trade. Field training is required in almost every situation, to ensure not just safety but survival.

Newly arrived field researchers learn a few simple lessons: change their sweaty socks so their feet don't freeze. And complicated ones: how to assess whether a chasm or crevasse can be safely crossed by a scientist on skis, a snowmobile, or a tractor. And challenging ones: how to get out of a deep hole in the ice, how to keep from freezing atop of a frozen mountain, and how to stay warm in a sleeping bag (hint: take a pee bottle to bed instead of a hot water bottle).

Field camping scientists learn to safely set up their camps, including pitching tents, operating stoves, and establishing toilet procedures with pee bottles and "shewees" (pee bottles shaped for women), pee barrels (to empty the bottles into), and poop buckets for everyone. What's more, camps must establish a survival cache (a secure, hidden store of supplies) upwind from the camp to keep it safe if the camp catches fire, equipping it with two to four weeks' worth of food, clothing, sleeping and cooking gear, first aid, a VHF (very high frequency) radio, and lanterns for everyone in their party.

Out in the field, it's not just the weather that's out for blood, it's the terrain. Mountaineers teach researchers field survival skills, such as how to build shelters: snow trenches, igloos, and snow caves, or "quinzees." Researchers learn how to pull a cargo sled loaded with two-person Scott tents through uneven or crevassed areas; how to climb a rope in bulbous "bunny" boots; and how to fix a stalled snowmobile. Every participant in field camping sites must learn how to "hold" a fall by hacking into ice with an ice axe, how to get out of a crevasse, how to rappel down a cliff or climb down to a victim and hoist him or her out of the ice, and how to perform advanced first aid.

SCOTT TENT

This tent, seen at field stations all over Antarctica, was named (again) for Captain Robert Falcon Scott, who invented it for his 1910–13 South Pole Expedition. The tent can withstand the 62 mph (100 kmph) katabatic winds (strong gusts forced down the slope of the Transantarctic Mountains by gravity). Just as importantly, it "breathes out" the water vapor that forms when the campers breathe, so it doesn't condense on the inside of the tent and drip freezing water onto their heads. And it weighs just 66 pounds (30 kg), making it relatively easy to transport.

Inside a Scott tent

POLAR SOLAR

Surviving in the field means bringing the right gear. You might be surprised to learn how important suntan lotion and sunglasses are in the Antarctic environment, where so many surfaces are reflective, multiplying the sunlight, which shines for the majority of the day. High-SPF lotion helps prevent sunburn, and dark-coated sunglasses that shield the eyes at every angle keep you from going sunblind, which is the result of eye damage from too much bright light.

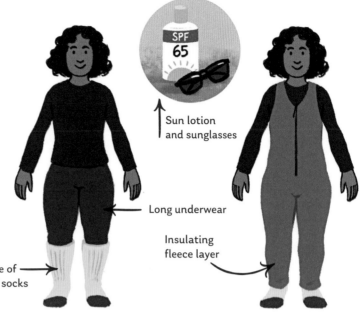

Sun lotion and sunglasses

Long underwear

A couple of pairs of socks

Insulating fleece layer

Sweater or fleece

Snowpants

Layers of lightweight jackets and tops

Hand warmers in gloves

Balaclava helmet that covers your face

Parka

Foot warmers in boots

Flotation jacket (if you're boating)

Fur mitts, sometimes called "bear paws"

Thermal boots

For scientists working on boats, survival skills are different. For one thing, they're required to stay at least 1,000 feet (about 300 m) from icebergs, which can suddenly flip or break, putting boats and those onboard in danger. Brash ice, small close-set chunks of ice, can be dangerous if it sweeps out to sea, carrying a small boat along with it. And what happens if a storm sets in, if boaters get lost, or if a leopard seal bites a hole in the inflatable hull and air starts seeping out the bottom? Not only do boating scientists carry survival packs that include food, extra clothing, and other necessities, but they learn to locate survival caches on islands or remote parts of the coast. These containers have food, water, clothing, a stove, and other items designed to keep them alive until they can be rescued.

As for scuba divers, each boat or ice-hole team includes monitors—people that do nothing but stare into the sea and watch the flow of bubbles from each diver. The boat carries a horn to sound in case of danger and every diver knows how to make a letter L with their thumb and forefinger and hold it on top of their head, which means "leopard seal nearby!" What's more, dive teams are trained in emergency medical procedures.

Many station personnel are emergency medical technicians or know emergency first aid. Among the most prized and carefully trained groups at any station is the fire squad. Imagine what would happen if fire spread throughout a station. This has happened a few times, including at Russia's Mirny station in 2020. Winds helped the fire spread from the weather station, where it started, to several labs, before it could be extinguished.

Scientists crossing the ice on snowmobiles or other vehicles need to keep a sharp eye out for melt pools that form on top of the ice, as well as seal holes, cracks, and crevasses. It's not enough to trust the tracks of a vehicle that has already traveled through the area, as conditions change quickly: travelers must stop and drill small holes in the ice to assess its thickness, and never travel across ice thinner than 30 inches (75 cm)—even thicker for larger, heavier vehicles.

And it almost goes without saying that anyone leaving a station or camp carries along a high-frequency radio, signs out, and signs back in, because if they don't, a search party will set out to find them.

1st South Pole station

2nd South Pole station

3rd South Pole station

A POLE APART

Think back to the heroic explorers of a century ago. Which of them could imagine that people would one day live and work at the South Pole all year round? But it's true. While those who have been to "the ice" of Antarctica consider themselves part of an exclusive club, there's special respect for workers of every stripe who "winter over," dealing with the coldest, darkest conditions anywhere—especially at the Amundsen-Scott South Pole Station (U.S.), the very bottom of the world.

They just call it "Pole." The station sits on top of a 9,000-feet (2,700-m)-thick plateau of ice that drifts 33 feet (10 m) a year. A permanent research station was established there in 1956–57 but is now buried. It was replaced in 1975 by a geodesic dome structure, which was dismantled and removed in 2009–10, leaving the Pole to the new, third station. At peak capacity, it houses 150 people.

Most arrive here from McMurdo Station via LC-130 planes, but there is another way: the South Pole Traverse, known as SPoT. Three times a year, this parade of tractors hauls fuel over the 1,000-mile (1,600-km) route from McMurdo Station to the South Pole. At the front, a tracked vehicle pushing a radar boom senses the ice for fractures that could endanger the tractor train. Farther back, a car containing the living quarters and kitchen for the crew is hauled by a tractor of its own.

The South Pole's desert-dry, crystal-clear, and fiercely freezing air makes it the best spot on the planet for looking deep into the universe to study scarcely detectable particles and cosmic rays. Astrophysicists working here research light waves still being sent out from the Big Bang that began our universe 13.8 billion years ago. The IceCube experiment picks up the signals of neutrinos, minute particles that travel through space. Here, at the bottom of the world, scientists are harnessing Antarctica's unique environment to study the greatest mysteries of the universe.

LEAVING ANTARCTICA

Working in Antarctica, it's easy to feel as small as a tiny krill getting sucked into a bottle dropped from a small boat: what difference does one small piece of data, one small scientist (or writer) make? The answer is that each small piece goes a long way in opening the window not just on how Antarctica works, but also on the entire world. Each person—and each piece of information they gather—adds to that story. And there's plenty more to find out, plenty more room in Antarctica for the next generation of Antarcticans, plenty more windows to be opened to understand this amazing continent. Go, if you possibly can.

When I left Antarctica with my team and headed back north, back home, I cried. I packed my notebooks, art supplies, hats, socks, mittens, and the big red parka I had to return when we made it back across the Drake Passage to Punta Arenas. At last I stood on the *Laurence M. Gould* with Pete, Paty, Carlton, and new friends I'd met on the ship and at Palmer Station. My heart ached for the people and place I was leaving. Palmer Station stood glowing under a gloomy, dark autumn sky (by the time we left there were just four hours of light a day) with snow falling. Sniff!

But something sweet happened as our ship steamed away from the wharf where once I'd stared into a leopard seal's eyes: the winter people—the scientists and support crew left behind—ran down to the wharf and leaped into the icy waters of Hero Inlet. Cold! Crazy! And kind. It's a gesture meant to wish the ship a safe crossing, to wish those aboard a return to the ice, and it made us laugh through our tears.

I went back to Antarctica the next year, but the icebergs there were so thick the ship never made it within 100 miles of the coast (like Captain Cook!). Since arriving home, I haven't stopped writing about Antarctica for a single week, and I've joined those who've made it their lives' work to tell its story—and to share information about climate change. We owe it to the Earth to try to save it. Worldwide, millions of people are working on new laws, international agreements, and farming and energy innovations to protect our planet. They are led by teenagers, most of whom have never seen the ice but who know what global warming means for Antarctica. It may be hard to reverse the shrinking of the Antarctic ice, but it's possible.

I don't know if I'll ever get back to Antarctica, but I intend to try. It's true what they say: it's a harsh continent. But it's also true that once the ice gets into your blood, Antarctica stays in your heart.

GLOSSARY

CLIMATE
The long-term conditions that characterize an environment regularly. For example, climates may be tropical, temperate (or seasonal), or glacial. Climate is often compared against weather, which instead means the short-term changes in the atmosphere.

CORE (SEDIMENT OR ICE)
A cylinder drilled up either from the ground (including at the bottom of the ocean) or from an ice sheet. Sediment cores pull up ancient soil, sand, rock, and the remains of plants and animals. Ice cores pull up ancient ice containing rock and air pockets from long ago. Studying either of these is a window on the past.

CREVASSE
A long, deep crack in a glacier or other ice that can be dangerous to humans or animals.

CURRENT
A river in the sea that is set apart from the waters around it by its temperature, density, speed, or chemical characteristics (such as saltiness).

FOSSIL
The ancient remains of an animal that died long ago and was preserved in soil, ice, or rock.

HEMISPHERE
One half of Earth. The Northern and Southern hemispheres are divided along the equator, the 0° latitude line, while the Eastern and Western hemispheres are divided at the Greenwich Meridian, the 0° longitude line.

ICEBREAKER
A ship specially designed for breaking through thick ice. These ships have reinforced hulls, powerful engines, and a special shape to help them push through the ice. Icebreakers can be used to clear channels through the ice that other ships can pass through.

IGLOO
A structure built out of snow for shelter and warmth. Compacted snow is cut into blocks and then stacked to form a dome-shaped shelter. The snow traps the heat within, so the igloo keeps anyone inside safe from the cold. Building igloos is a tradition that originates with indigenous Inuit people from the Arctic Circle and North America.

INHOSPITABLE
Without conditions that support life.

NEUTRINO
A subatomic (smaller than an atom) particle with almost no mass and no electrical charge. Because of these attributes, neutrinos pass through things easily and are very hard to detect.

PLANKTON
Any of the tiny living things found in water. Plankton in the water can include single-celled bacteria, algae, microscopic animals, and many other groups. They are a key food source for many marine creatures, from tiny krill to huge whales.

QUINZEE
A snow shelter similar to an igloo but instead built from a pile of snow that is then hollowed out (rather than from snow bricks).

SUBMERSIBLE
A small vehicle designed to travel underwater. Submersibles may have a crew on board or be controlled remotely, in which case they are known as remotely operated vehicles (ROVs).

WINTERING OVER
Term used for staying in Antarctica over the winter. This time is particularly tough on the continent due to extremely low temperatures, constant darkness, and the lack of any way off the continent until summer.

SOURCE NOTES

This book was developed through extensive research, interviews with scientists in Antarctica, reviews by experts in the continent, as well as my own travel notes. It would be impossible to list all the sources used, but here are some places to look for more information about this incredible continent.

- Karen Romano Young

. . . .

Armstrong, J. *Shipwreck at the Bottom of the World: The Extraordinary Story of Shackleton and the Endurance.* Crown, 1998

"Blood as White as Snow" broadcast. March 1, 2019. *Science Friday.* https://www.sciencefriday.com/segments/this-antarctic-fish-has-blood-as-white-as-snow/

"Antarctic Stations — Currently Occupied," *Cool Antarctica.* https://www.coolantarctica.com/Community/antarctic_bases.php

Cumming, V. "When dinosaurs roamed Antarctica," *BBC Earth.* https://www.bbcearth.com/blog/?article=when-dinosaurs-roamed-antarctica

"Impacts of Climate Change," *Discovering Antarctica.* British Antarctic Survey. https://discoveringantarctica.org.uk/challenges/sustainability/impacts-of-climate-change/

Fox, A. "The northern and southern lights are different. Here's why." January 25, 2019. *Science.* https://www.sciencemag.org/news/2019/01/northern-and-southern-lights-are-different-here-s-why

Grill, W. *Shackleton's Journey.* Flying Eye Books, London, 2014

"Halley VI Research Station" video. January 15, 2014. British Antarctic Survey. https://www.youtube.com/watch?time_continue=4&v=dhR-JZLtzvQ&feature=emb_logo

Hegyi, F. "Life at Palmer Station, Antarctica" video, October 28, 2018. https://www.youtube.com/watch?v=SBZhgfSVirA&t=32s

International Thwaites Glacier Collaboration. https://thwaitesglacier.org

"The Last Husky: The Final Journey of Antarctica's Sledge Dogs" video. https://www.youtube.com/watch?v=lGr6MxmKCkQ&t=4s

Lucibella, M. "The South Pole Traverse: Convoy to the Bottom of the Planet" podcast. May 20, 2019. *Antarctic Sun.* https://antarcticsun.usap.gov/features/4397/

"Hunt for the Giant Squid" NHK Documentary. *Nat Geo Wild.* https://www.nationalgeographic.com/tv/movies-and-specials/hunt-for-the-giant-squid

Oskin, B. "What Antarctica Looked Like Before the Ice," March 7, 2013. *Live Science.* https://www.livescience.com/27715-antarctica-before-ice.html

Powell, H. "On the Antarctic Peninsula, Scientists Witness a Bird Revolution," January 26, 2016. *All About Birds*, Cornell University website. https://www.allaboutbirds.org/news/on-the-antarctic-peninsula-scientists-witness-a-penguin-revolution/

Saildrone website. https://www.saildrone.com

Southern Ocean Carbon and Climate Observation and Modeling project. https://soccom.princeton.edu

"Surviving Earth's Extremes: How Antarctic Animals Freeze and Reanimate" video, Brigham Young University. https://www.youtube.com/watch?v=gLDTdonElbO

INDEX

ABOUT THE AUTHOR AND ILLUSTRATOR

Karen Romano Young is a polar explorer, deep sea diver, writer, illustrator, and science comics creator. She has three children, two grandchildren, a husband, and a gigantic black and white dog.

Angela Hsieh is an illustrator, writer, and erstwhile biology student. She shares her apartment with a polydactyl cat. She once visited Antarctica and can confirm that penguins are indeed adorable and awfully smelly.